James A. Garfield

JAMES A. *Garfield*

OUR TWENTIETH PRESIDENT

By Carol Brunelli

SPIRIT
of America™

The Child's World®, Inc.
Chanhassen, Minnesota

7

JAMES A. *Garfield*

Published in the United States of America by The Child's World®, Inc.
PO Box 326 • Chanhassen, MN 55317-0326 • 800-599-READ • www.childsworld.com

Acknowledgments

The Creative Spark: Mary Francis-DeMarois, Project Director; Elizabeth Sirimarco Budd, Series Editor; Robert Court, Design and Art Direction; Janine Graham, Page Layout; Jennifer Moyers, Production

The Child's World®, Inc.: Mary Berendes, Publishing Director; Red Line Editorial, Fact Research; Cindy Klingel, Curriculum Advisor; Robert Noyed, Historical Advisor

Photos:

Cover: White House Collection, courtesy White House Historical Association; Lake County Historical Society, Mentor, Ohio: 6, 7, 9, 10, 12, 13, 14, 20, 22, 24; Library of Congress: 15, 17, 19, 23, 26, 27, 28, 29, 30, 31, 34; North Wind Picture Archives: 32, 36, 37; Paul A. Souders/CORBIS: 8; Rutherford B. Hayes Presidential Center, Fremont, OH: 25

Registration

The Child's World®, Inc., Spirit of America™, and their associated logos are the sole property and registered trademarks of The Child's World®, Inc.

Library of Congress Cataloging-in-Publication Data
Brunelli, Carol.
James A. Garfield, our twentieth president / Carol Brunelli.
p. cm.
Includes bibliographical references and index.
ISBN 1-56766-857-7
1. Garfield, James A. (James Abram), 1831–1881—Juvenile literature. 2. Presidents—United States—Biography—Juvenile literature. [1.Garfield, James A. (James Abram), 1831–1881.
2. Presidents.] I. Title.
E687 .B88 2001
973.8'4'092—dc21

00-011456

Contents

Chapter ONE

Teacher and Preacher

James Garfield rose from life as a poor boy from rural Ohio to become the president of the United States. As a young man, he worked hard to achieve his goals. His friends and family were sure he had a promising future.

JAMES ABRAM GARFIELD WAS THE YOUNGEST of Abram and Eliza Garfield's five children. He was born in a log cabin near Cleveland, Ohio, on November 19, 1831. James was just two years old when his father died, and his mother was left to raise the children alone. Eliza was strong and religious, and she worked hard to keep the farm and the family together. She taught her children important lessons about life.

James grew up with very little money, but he knew how to work hard for a better life. His poverty embarrassed him many times in his youth, but he later gained respect for what he achieved in spite of it. His mother's faith helped him realize that he could achieve great things with his life, even though he grew up poor.

At age 16, James left home in search of adventure. He had always dreamed of becoming a sailor, so he went to the Cleveland waterfront. There he found a job as a canal boy. His main duty was to lead the horses that pulled barges along the Ohio and Pennsylvania Canal, a waterway used to transport goods and people. Strangely enough, James couldn't swim! He fell into the canal many times, but he was always

Garfield was born in this simple log cabin in a part of Ohio known as the Western Reserve. The area was mostly forest at the time, but it was soon filled with homes and dairy farms.

Like this man, Garfield worked on the canals of Ohio, leading horses and mules that pulled barges along the waterway.

saved by one of the lines that pulled the horses along. After six months of near misses, James decided the life of a sailor wasn't for him and headed home. On the way, he came down with a serious fever. It lasted for nearly five months.

By March of 1849, James was healthy again. He decided to reach for another dream. As a young boy, he had learned to read and write at a schoolhouse near his home, but he wanted more education. James enrolled at a school called the Geauga Academy. His family still had little money, so he worked his way through school by doing farm chores. He also taught some of the courses after he had completed them.

At his new school, James learned to love **debating.** This interest would last throughout his life. It helped him become an excellent public speaker after he entered **politics.** In his studies, James always did careful research on topics that interested him. This habit of careful study also helped him succeed.

By the fall of 1850, James was ready for college. He entered Western Reserve Eclectic Institute (now called Hiram College). At college, he discovered that he was a great public speaker. People liked to listen to him. He started **preaching** when he joined a church called the Disciples of Christ. He would continue to preach at church until he entered Congress in 1863.

After the death of her husband, Eliza Garfield raised her children by herself. James felt close to his mother throughout his life. As an adult, he remembered that her wisdom had guided him at every important moment in his life.

James preached nearly every Sunday while he taught at the Eclectic Institute. Hundreds gathered to hear him. In 1854, he entered Williams College in Massachusetts. There he joined debating groups, arguing about the issues of the day. One classmate described him as "undoubtedly one of the greatest debaters ever seen at Williams … [he] won and held the attention of this

Garfield (at far left) taught a Greek class at the Western Reserve Eclectic Institute. He posed for this photograph with his students, including his future wife, Lucretia, who is seated beside him.

audience from the moment he opened his lips." James graduated from Williams with honors in 1856. He returned to the Eclectic Institute and became its president.

In 1858, James married one of his former students, Lucretia Rudolph, whom he called "Crete." He began to realize that he did not want to spend the rest of his life as an educator. "My heart will never be satisfied to spend my life in teaching," he once wrote to a friend. "I think there are other fields in which a man can do more."

About this time, James became interested in politics. He also began to speak out against slavery, the most difficult problem the nation faced at the time. Slavery threatened the future of the nation because many people in the northern states wanted to end it. But people in the southern states were not willing to lose the free labor the slaves provided. Southerners threatened to **secede** from United States if slavery was outlawed. They said they would create their own country. Like many people who opposed slavery, James supported the Republican Party, one of the two major **political parties** of the day.

Garfield cared a great deal for Lucretia Rudolph. But for many years, he could not make up his mind to marry. They dated for a long time before they wed in 1858. Many years later, he wrote in his diary about how happy he was in his marriage. "If I could write out the story of Crete's life and mine," he wrote, "it would be a more wonderful record than any I know in the realm of romance."

By 1859, James had turned his love for preaching and teaching into a political career. He decided to run for the Ohio State Senate. He was an excellent **candidate** because he was already well known to people in his hometown. Every time he gave a speech, James spoke out firmly against slavery. He was elected to the Ohio State Senate less than two years before the **Civil War** would divide the nation.

AN ELDERLY FRIEND GAVE GARFIELD THE FOLLOWING rules for living. Garfield tried to follow them until the end of his life.

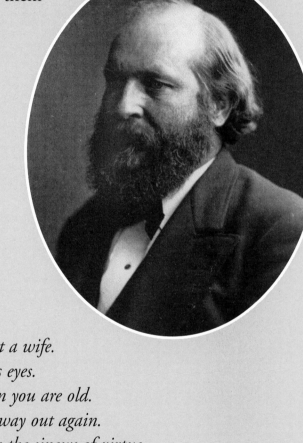

Never be idle.
Make few promises.
Always speak the truth.
Live within your income.
Never speak evil of anyone.
Keep good company or none.
Live up to your engagements.
Never play games of chance.
Drink no intoxicating [alcoholic] drinks.
Good character is above everything else.
Keep your own secrets if you have any.
Never borrow if you can possibly help it.
Do not marry until you are able to support a wife.
When you speak to a person, look into his eyes.
Save when you are young and spend when you are old.
Never run into debt unless you can see a way out again.
Good company and good conversation are the sinews of virtue.
Your character cannot be essentially injured except by your own acts.
If anybody speaks evil of you, let your life be so that no one believes him.
When you retire at night think over what you have done during the day.
If your hands cannot be employed usefully, attend to the culture of your mind.
Read the above carefully and thoughtfully at least once a week.

Chapter TWO

Soldier and Congressman

Garfield volunteered to fight for the Union army shortly after the South formed the Confederate States of America.

ABRAHAM LINCOLN WAS ELECTED PRESIDENT in November of 1860. Within seven months, eleven Southern states had left the **Union** and formed their own nation, which they called the **Confederate** States of America. They refused to support a president who they believed would work to end slavery. It seemed that the United States was about to fall apart.

In a letter to an old friend, Garfield wrote, "I do not see any way, outside a miracle of God, which can avoid civil war with all its attendant horrors." Garfield was right. The country was soon at war. The Union did not have an army ready to fight. President Lincoln called on the states for 75,000 soldiers. Garfield was one of the men who volunteered to fight for the Union forces.

From the beginning, he favored freedom for the slaves.

During the Civil War, Garfield quickly rose in **rank**. He entered the army as a lieutenant colonel. Just a few months later, he was promoted to the rank of colonel, in charge of the 42nd Ohio Volunteer Regiment. His first battlefield assignment was at the head of a brigade, which is a large group of soldiers. The brigade was sent to fight in Kentucky. It included the 42nd Regiment.

The Civil War began on April 12, 1861, when the Confederates bombed Fort Sumter, a Union fort off the coast of South Carolina.

15

Garfield and his brigade were successful. They pushed the Confederates out of Kentucky. By 1862, Colonel Garfield was **promoted** to the rank of brigadier general, an important position in the army. He left his regiment and led another brigade in the Shiloh and Corinth **campaigns.** At the Battle of Shiloh, Garfield wrote about what he saw in a letter to his wife: "The horrible sights I have witnessed on this field, I can never describe."

Garfield (center) was a great soldier, and the army recognized his skill. He was promoted to the rank of major general before he left the army to take his seat in Congress.

In November of 1862, Garfield was elected to the House of Representatives, which is part of the U.S. Congress. He was still in the army at the time. Although Garfield was a dedicated soldier, he left the army to do his job as a congressman in Washington, D.C. President Lincoln helped Garfield make this decision. He told him that it was easier to find good generals than to find good Republicans for Congress. But before Garfield entered Congress, the army honored him once more by making him a major general.

When Garfield became a congressman, the dome of the U.S. Capitol was still under construction.

▶ In 1863, Congress-
man Garfield left
Washington to see his
wife. When he arrived
home, Mrs. Garfield
handed him a sheet of
paper on which she
had summed up their
life together up to that
time. They had been
married for nearly
five years, but they
had lived together for
only 20 weeks. Garfield
promised then and
there that he would
never again go to Wash-
ington without her.

Garfield took a short rest, returning to Ohio to be with his wife, their daughter Eliza, and their infant son Harry. Soon after Garfield's arrival, young Eliza died. Garfield left for the nation's capital city without his family. He felt sad and lonely as he entered the U.S. Congress in 1863. By the beginning of the next session, he had brought his family to Washington, where they would live throughout his career in politics.

The Civil War ended in 1865. The South had lost, and the slaves were freed. But the nation now had new problems to face. People worried about what would become of the former slaves. No one knew exactly how the **freedpeople** would support themselves. No one knew how to protect them from Southerners who still believed African Americans should be slaves. The nation also faced the difficult job of reconstructing, or rebuilding, the South. The government had to decide how much power to give the states that had **rebelled** against the Union. This era in U.S. history is known as Reconstruction.

Garfield joined the Radical Republicans, a group of Northern Republicans who wanted a severe form of reconstruction in the South.

The Radical Republicans were determined that the ex-Confederates should suffer and struggle before they could rejoin the United States. Many Radical Republicans also supported suffrage, or the right to vote, for black men. Garfield voted for the Civil Rights Act of 1866, which gave U.S. citizenship to the freedpeople. But he did not believe that giving voting rights to blacks was enough to save the South. He believed education was the key to success for all Americans, black or white, Northern or Southern.

Garfield supported equal educational opportunities for blacks. He also supported the creation of a national Department of Education, which would oversee the creation of public schools. He supported educating deaf people and creating the museums of the

Garfield was a member of Congress for 17 years. He gained a reputation as a friendly and thoughtful man, and eventually became the most powerful Republican in the House of Representatives.

19

Garfield and his family were avid readers. This picture, taken while he was a member of Congress, shows him reading to his daughter Mary.

Smithsonian Institution. Garfield also backed the creation of the U.S. Geological Survey. This government agency identifies land, water, energy, and mineral **resources.** It also creates maps and investigates hazards, such as earthquakes and volcanoes.

Garfield served in the U.S. House of Representatives from 1863 to 1880. During his many years in Congress, he became the most important Republican in the House. He was an expert on financial and educational issues. He served on many committees, such as the Committee on Banking and Currency and the Committee on the **Census.** He believed that collecting information about the American public with a census was important. It would allow the U.S. government to create better programs and services for its people. Many of Garfield's ideas were included in the 1880 census. Today the

Census Bureau gathers information about the American people on many topics, such as health and education.

Garfield also believed that currency, or paper money, should be backed by gold. This means that the government would have gold **reserves** equal to the amount of currency that Americans were using. During the Civil War, the government printed more money than usual to help pay for the war. Dollars were worth less than before because there wasn't enough gold for each dollar. The Gold Act was finally passed in 1900, 19 years after Garfield had died.
But many people said that Garfield supported this act more than any other politician and helped it become a reality.

In January of 1880, Garfield was elected to the U.S. Senate. He would have little time to devote to the position. Later that year, the Republican Party chose him as their presidential candidate for the election of 1880. Chester A. Arthur was chosen as his running mate.

When elections came in November, Garfield beat the Democratic candidate, General Winfield Scott Hancock, by only

10,000 popular votes (the votes of the American people). It was the closest popular election up to that time. Afterward, Garfield received a letter from another future president from Ohio, Benjamin Harrison. He wrote to congratulate Garfield, saying, "Outside your family, I am sure no man in the country can be happier than I am over your elevation to the presidency."

AFTER THE CIVIL War ended, the lives of former slaves, called freedpeople, were still terribly difficult. Most Southern blacks were illiterate, which means they could not read or write. When they tried to find jobs in factories, white workers complained that freedpeople were stealing their jobs. Many of the freedpeople wanted to own farms, but white landowners refused to sell them land. Others would not rent land to former slaves or give them bank loans. As a result, African Americans had no choice but to work for white farmers. Usually, they barely earned enough money to feed their families. The new lives of the freedpeople seemed little better than slavery. James Garfield wanted to improve this situation. He said, "We have seen white men betray the flag and fight to kill the Union, but all that long, dreary war, we never saw a traitor in black skin."

After the Civil War ended in 1865, Garfield voted for black suffrage. He also supported equal educational opportunities for blacks. When he became president in 1881, Garfield also made sure to give government jobs to African Americans.

Chapter THREE

Stalwarts versus Half-Breeds

Although Garfield won the presidential election of 1880 by only a small number of votes, Americans admired him. They respected the fact that he came from a humble background, succeeding through hard work and intelligence.

MANY AMERICANS WERE HAPPY WHEN JAMES A. Garfield became the 20th president in 1881. He was a successful politician because he was hardworking and honest, which is what Americans wanted in their most important representative. He once said, "The people are responsible for the character of their Congress. If that body be ignorant, reckless, and corrupt, it is because the people tolerate ignorance, recklessness, and corruption. If it be intelligent, brave, and pure, it is because the people demand these high qualities to represent them." What Garfield meant is this: It is up to American voters to choose the best people for their government. If the nation's leaders are not honest or good, it is the fault of those who voted for them. The work Garfield did as a

congressman and later as president proved that Americans had chosen a good representative.

As soon as Garfield was elected president, he found himself in the middle of a dangerous struggle for power. Two **factions** had formed within the Republican Party. They were called the Stalwarts and the Half-Breeds. These two groups were fighting each other for positions in the new president's government. The Republicans had split into these factions more

Interesting Facts

▶ Garfield's 80-year-old mother, Eliza Garfield, was the first mother of a president to attend her son's inauguration.

▶ Snow on the ground kept many people from attending Garfield's inauguration at the U.S. Capitol.

25

than four years earlier, during the election of 1876. They split because they could not agree on a presidential candidate. The Stalwarts, led by Senator Roscoe Conkling of New York, wanted former president Ulysses S. Grant to run for a third term. Garfield had joined the second faction, which supported Senator James G. Blaine of Maine. A third candidate, Republican Rutherford B. Hayes, won the nomination and the election. But the two factions still fought with each other. The Stalwarts nicknamed Blaine's supporters "half-breeds," which meant that they were not true Republicans.

One task that President Garfield faced as soon as he entered office was to fill many government jobs. Hundreds of people lined up outside the White House looking for a position. Again and again, the White House staff had to turn away visitors to the mansion. The line of people waiting to see the president stretched all the way to the street. "I received several thousand in the East Room," remembered Garfield.

Problems between the Stalwarts and the Half-Breeds grew worse as soon as the president started choosing people for certain jobs. Each faction wanted the president to choose its members.

At first, the Stalwarts were pleased when the president recommended some of them for positions, even though Garfield himself was a Half-Breed. But a struggle developed when Garfield's **secretary of state,** James Blaine, tried to replace several Stalwarts with Half-Breeds. Blaine wanted Half-Breed William H. Robertson to replace Stalwart Edwin A. Merritt as the collector of the port of New York. This position collected taxes on imports, which are goods brought into the United States from other countries. It was an important job because the port of New York handled more imports and collected more money than all other U.S. ports combined.

Senator Conkling complained, and the president tried to **compromise.** He promised

Garfield chose James Blaine (below) as his secretary of state. Like Garfield, Blaine was part of the Half-Breed faction. He had hoped to be a presidential candidate four years earlier, but the Republicans chose Rutherford B. Hayes instead.

Conkling that Merritt would remain the collector. But Garfield also told Conkling that Robertson would be appointed to position as well. Senator Conkling would not compromise—he did not want Robertson to have any position at all. The president grew tired of the tug-of-war between the factions, and he was angry about Conkling's stubbornness. Garfield made a decision: Robertson would get the position as collector. The Senate approved this choice, in part because the senators were pleased that Garfield had stood up to Conkling.

Garfield's showdown with Conkling impressed the public. It proved to Americans that no single person has the right to decide who will be an employee of the U.S. government—not an important person like Senator Conkling or even the president. Garfield made his choices for government positions, but then the Senate decided whether to accept them.

As a young man, Garfield had enjoyed socializing and going out on the town. But as he grew older, he valued time with his family. As a congressman and then as president, he found Washington's social life "uncomfortable and meaningless." He preferred to stay at home reading or playing cards.

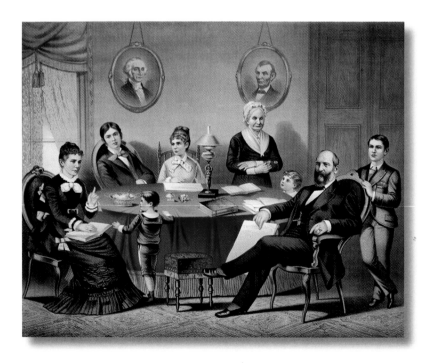

ON APRIL 16, 1865, THE DAY AFTER ABRAHAM LINCOLN DIED, WORD BEGAN
to spread about what had happened. The Civil War had just ended, and the
country was tense and afraid. The United States had lost one of the greatest
leaders in its history. Americans wondered what would happen next.

Garfield was in New York City that day. He came upon a crowd of about
50,000 people. Two men were lying in the street. They had been shot, and one
of them was dead. Apparently, they had spoken against Lincoln and were shot
by someone in the angry mob that had formed. The crowd was furious and
seemed to be prepared for more violence. Garfield stepped into the crowd to
calm them down. Soon he raised his right arm and began to preach. He sympa-
thized with their fears. He assured them that their government was still strong
and healthy. "Fellow citizens," he said, "God reigns and the government at
Washington still lives."

Chapter FOUR

Tragedy in Washington

Garfield had many years of experience in politics. People believed he would do great things during his presidency. Unfortunately, he would have little time to achieve his goals.

BY STANDING UP TO CONKLING AND THE Stalwarts, Garfield showed both his opponents and the American people that he was a strong president. He proved that he would make his own decisions, even if members of his own political party disagreed with him.

Garfield wanted to do great things, but he did not have much time to achieve his goals. He would serve only about 200 days as president. Garfield did have success in this short time, however. Soon after he took office, he learned about a problem in the U.S. Postal Service. There were complaints that certain mail delivery routes, called the "Star Routes," were being run in a dishonest way. Star Routes delivered mail to faraway areas of the South and the West where mail

could not be delivered by train or steamship. The federal government made private contracts with horse, stagecoach, and wagon agencies to deliver mail to these areas.

By 1880, there were 9,225 Star Routes, which cost almost $6 million to run. They were so expensive because some agencies tricked the U.S. government. They received the routes by charging a lower price than

This political cartoon shows Garfield's adviser, Thomas Brady, holding a bag of stars that symbolize the Star Routes of the Postal Service. Garfield was disappointed to learn that one of his advisors was involved in dishonest activities.

other agencies. Once they had control of the route, the agencies claimed that they had improved their service and needed more money. Sometimes they even charged for routes that did not exist.

The government decided to investigate the Star Routes. It discovered that members of both the Postal Service and of the Republican Party were involved in the dishonest actions. In fact, even one of Garfield's advisers, Thomas Brady, was involved. Six weeks later, the president asked Brady to leave his position. Garfield would not stand for dishonesty among his aides.

As a congressman, Garfield had to deal with the nation's money matters. He continued to do this as president. He helped reduce the national debt, money that the country had borrowed and had to pay back. Garfield also wanted to improve the country's relations with Latin America. He asked Secretary of State Blaine to invite all nations in the Americas to a conference. It was supposed to take place in Washington in 1882. Unfortunately, the conference never took place. A terrible tragedy struck before it could be held.

After he became president, Garfield began to have nightmares about his own death. It was not the first time a president would have such terrible dreams. At a meeting, Garfield spoke with President Lincoln's son, Robert. Garfield asked him to describe the dreams his father had had just before he was **assassinated.** Lincoln explained that his father once dreamed of a dead body lying in the East Room of the White House. In the dream, Abraham heard someone crying. He asked a soldier standing guard, "Who is dead in the White House?" The soldier replied, "The president." Hearing this story disturbed President Garfield.

After breakfast on the morning of July 2, 1881, Secretary of State Blaine and President Garfield went to the railroad station in Washington. While walking to the train,

Charles J. Guiteau had planned to kill the president two weeks earlier on June 18, 1881. He followed Garfield to the train station, but decided not to shoot the president at that time. Mrs. Garfield was with her husband that day, and Guiteau said she "clung so tenderly to the president's arm that I did not have the heart to fire on him." Less than one month later, Guiteau fired two shots at Garfield.

Garfield was shot by a man named Charles J. Guiteau. The president had been in office for less than four months. Mr. Guiteau had supported Garfield during his election. He had even written a pamphlet to help him win. Guiteau hoped that Garfield would give him an important government position when he became president. When Garfield did not, Guiteau became angry and decided to kill him.

President Garfield did not die right away. At first, he was treated in the White House. An expensive air-conditioning system was installed to keep him cool in the sweltering summer heat. It used 100 pounds of ice each hour. Week after week, Americans waited to hear news about the president's condition. Garfield himself tried to reassure the public, saying, "It is true I am still weak, and on my back; but I am gaining every day, and need only time and patience to bring me through."

Two months after he was shot, the president seemed to be doing better. He asked to be moved to New Jersey, hoping to recover by the seashore. A team of 300 men laid a half-mile railroad track so that a special train could take the president right to the front door of his cottage by the sea. Unfortunately, Garfield's condition grew worse after he arrived in New Jersey.

On September 19, 1881, President James Abram Garfield died from infection and internal bleeding. His wife was by his side. The nation mourned, for Garfield had made the country better and stronger. He also left a good example for future presidents. He did not give in to powerful political parties. He did not accept dishonesty in the government.

In 1879, writer Albion W. Tourgee wrote a book called *Figs and Thistles*. Many believed this book was about the life of James Abram Garfield. It was a story of a poor, fatherless boy who worked his way through school and grew up to be president of the United States. Tourgee's story had a happy ending. Unfortunately, Garfield's story did not. But this preacher, teacher, and leader gave the country hope for an honest government and a strong nation.

Railroad workers labored through the night to build a special railroad that would take the president right to the door of his seaside cottage.

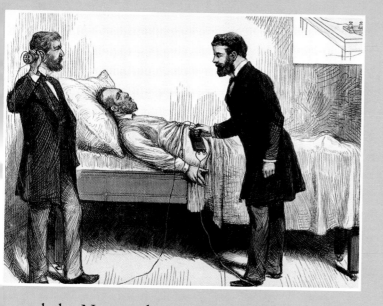

JAMES GARFIELD LIVED FOR MORE than two months after he was shot. Doctors tried many times to take out the bullet that was lodged in his chest, but they couldn't find it. Two scientists, Simon Newcomb and Alexander Graham Bell, tried to help. Newcomb was experimenting with running electricity through wire coils. He found that when metal was placed near the coils, he could hear a faint hum. He hoped to perfect his invention so that it could be used to locate the bullet.

Bell read about Newcomb in a newspaper. He offered his help, suggesting that his invention, the telephone, might be able to improve Newcomb's invention. It could make the humming sound louder. The two men joined forces and came up with an early version of a metal detector.

On July 26, Bell and Newcomb went to the White House to try their invention. The detector made a humming sound no matter where it was placed on the president's body. Bell and Newcomb left the White House confused and disappointed. Why didn't their invention work?

Bell returned to the lab with Newcomb. They ran more experiments, and their invention worked well. They returned to the White House on the last day of July. The same thing happened again. No matter where they placed the detector on the president's body, a faint hum could be heard.

What was wrong with Bell and Newcomb's invention? The invention wasn't the problem. The problem was the president's bed! It had springs made of metal, so the metal detector kept humming and humming. The White House was one of the few places that had mattresses with metal springs at the time. If Bell and Newcomb had moved the president off the bed and onto the floor, their invention could have found the bullet. James Garfield might have lived!

1831 James A. Garfield is born on November 19 in northern Ohio. His home is in an area called the Western Reserve.

1833 Garfield's father dies, leaving Eliza Garfield to raise the children and run the family farm.

1848 Garfield leaves home to become a canal boy on the Cleveland waterfront.

1849 In March, Garfield begins taking classes at Geauga Academy. He teaches and takes carpentry jobs to pay for school.

1850 Garfield enters Western Reserve Eclectic Institute (now called Hiram College). He joins a church called the Disciples of Christ and begins preaching.

1854 Garfield enters Williams College.

1856 Garfield graduates from Williams College and becomes a professor at the Western Reserve Eclectic Institute. He teaches ancient languages and literature.

1857 Garfield becomes the president of the Western Reserve Eclectic Institute. He holds the position until 1861, when the Civil War begins.

1858 Garfield marries Lucretia "Crete" Randolph at her family's home.

1859 Garfield is elected to the Ohio State Senate. He also begins to study law.

1860 Abraham Lincoln is elected president. The Southern states begin to secede from the Union and form a new nation, the Confederate States of America.

1861 On April 12, Confederate cannons fire on Fort Sumter in South Carolina, and the Civil War begins. Garfield volunteers as a soldier for the Union army.

1862 Garfield is promoted to the rank of brigadier general. In November, he is elected to the House of Representatives. Soon after, he is named a major general of the 42nd Ohio Volunteer Regiment. He resigns from the army to take his seat in the House.

1865 Lincoln takes the oath of office on March 4 to begin his second term as president. On April 9, General Robert E. Lee surrenders. The Civil War soon ends. On April 14, Lincoln is shot by John Wilkes Booth at Ford's Theater. He dies the next morning. The Reconstruction era begins. Americans help rebuild the South, which suffered great losses during the war. The government begins deciding how much power the former Confederates will have in the U.S. government. Garfield joins forces with the Radical Republicans, who believe Southerners must be held responsible for the rebellion. He supports voting rights and education for African Americans.

1869 As a congressman, Garfield fights for the creation of a Census Bureau.

1877 Reconstruction ends.

1879 The U.S. Geological Survey is created, which Garfield has supported in the House of Representatives.

1880 Garfield is elected senator. He is then nominated as a Republican presidential candidate. He runs a "front-porch campaign" from his home in Mentor, Ohio. He wins the election in November.

1881 Garfield is sworn in as the 20th president of the United States on March 4. In office, he struggles with problems between different factions in the Republican Party. He also fights dishonest activities in the U.S. Postal Service and encourages better relations with Latin America. On July 2, Charles J. Guiteau shoots the president. Guiteau is a former supporter of Garfield who is angry that he did not receive a government job. Doctors cannot find the bullet lodged in Garfield's back. Inventors Alexander Graham Bell and Simon Newcomb use a metal detector hoping to locate it, but they fail. After 11 weeks, the president dies on September 19, 1881. Guiteau is hanged for assassinating the president.

assassinate (uh-SASS-ih-nayt)
Assassinate means to murder someone, especially a well-known person. President Garfield was the second president to be assassinated.

campaigns (kam-PAYNZ)
Campaigns are related activities aimed at achieving a special goal. For example, a campaign can be activities during a war aimed at taking over a specific region. A campaign also can be activities before an election aimed at helping a candidate win.

candidate (KAN-dih-det)
A candidate is a person running in an election. Garfield was a good candidate for U.S. Senate because he was well known.

census (SEN-sus)
A census is an official count of the people in a country or district. It is taken to find out the number of people in the area, their ages, what they do for a living, and other facts.

civil war (SIV-il WAR)
A civil war is fought between opposing groups of citizens within the same country. The American Civil War began after 11 southern states seceded from the Union.

compromise (KOM-pruh-myz)
A compromise is a way to settle a disagreement in which both sides give up part of what they want. Garfield tried to reach a compromise with Senator Conkling over government jobs.

Confederate (kun-FED-er-et)
Confederate refers to the slave states that left the Union in 1860 and 1861. The people of these states were called Confederates.

debating (deh-BAY-ting)
Debating means taking part in a contest in which opponents argue for opposite sides of an issue. Garfield enjoyed debating.

factions (FAK-shenz)
Factions are small groups within a bigger organization, such as a political party. The Stalwarts and the Half-Breeds were factions of the Republican Party.

freedpeople (FREED-pee-pul)
Freedpeople were African Americans who had been slaves before slavery became illegal. After the Civil War, it was difficult for freed-people to support themselves.

**political parties
(puh-LIT-ih-kul PAR-teez)**
Political parties are groups of people
who share similar ideas about how to
run a government. Garfield supported
the the Republican political party.

politics (PAWL-ih-tiks)
Politics refers to the actions and
practices of the government. Garfield
became interested in politics while he
was an educator.

preaching (PREE-ching)
Preaching is giving a speech on a
religious subject. Garfield started
preaching when he joined a church
in 1850.

promoted (pruh-MOH-ted)
People who are promoted receive a
more important job or position to
recognize their good work. The Union
army promoted Garfield to the rank
of major general.

rank (RANK)
A rank is a job level in the military.
Garfield quickly rose in rank during
the Civil War.

rebel (reh-BEL)
If people rebel, they fight against their
government. The Southern states
rebelled against the U.S. government,
causing the Civil War.

reserves (rih-SERVZ)
Reserves are valuable assets, such as
money or gold, that are saved for a special
reason. At one time, the U.S. government
had gold reserves that equaled the
amount of dollars in circulation.

resources (REE-sor-sez)
Resources are supplies of useful things,
such as minerals, water, or land. The
U.S. Geological Survey studies the
nation's natural resources.

secede (suh-SEED)
If a group secedes, it separates from
a larger group. Eleven Southern states
seceded from the Union between 1860
and 1861.

**secretary of state
(SEK-ruh-tair-ee OF STAYT)**
The secretary of state is a close advisor to
the president. He or she is involved with
the country's relations with other nations.

Union (YOON-yen)
The Union is another name for the United
States of America. During the Civil War,
the North was called the Union.

President	Birthplace	Life Span	Presidency	Political Party	First Lady
George Washington	Virginia	1732–1799	1789–1797	None	Martha Dandridge Custis Washington
John Adams	Massachusetts	1735–1826	1797–1801	Federalist	Abigail Smith Adams
Thomas Jefferson	Virginia	1743–1826	1801–1809	Democratic-Republican	widower
James Madison	Virginia	1751–1836	1809–1817	Democratic Republican	Dolley Payne Todd Madison
James Monroe	Virginia	1758–1831	1817–1825	Democratic Republican	Elizabeth Kortright Monroe
John Quincy Adams	Massachusetts	1767–1848	1825–1829	Democratic-Republican	Louisa Johnson Adams
Andrew Jackson	South Carolina	1767–1845	1829–1837	Democrat	widower
Martin Van Buren	New York	1782–1862	1837–1841	Democrat	widower
William H. Harrison	Virginia	1773–1841	1841	Whig	Anna Symmes Harrison
John Tyler	Virginia	1790–1862	1841–1845	Whig	Letitia Christian Tyler Julia Gardiner Tyler
James K. Polk	North Carolina	1795–1849	1845–1849	Democrat	Sarah Childress Polk

Our PRESIDENTS

President	Birthplace	Life Span	Presidency	Political Party	First Lady
Zachary Taylor	Virginia	1784–1850	1849–1850	Whig	Margaret Mackall Smith Taylor
Millard Fillmore	New York	1800–1874	1850–1853	Whig	Abigail Powers Fillmore
Franklin Pierce	New Hampshire	1804–1869	1853–1857	Democrat	Jane Means Appleton Pierce
James Buchanan	Pennsylvania	1791–1868	1857–1861	Democrat	never married
Abraham Lincoln	Kentucky	1809–1865	1861–1865	Republican	Mary Todd Lincoln
Andrew Johnson	North Carolina	1808–1875	1865–1869	Democrat	Eliza McCardle Johnson
Ulysses S. Grant	Ohio	1822–1885	1869–1877	Republican	Julia Dent Grant
Rutherford B. Hayes	Ohio	1822–1893	1877–1881	Republican	Lucy Webb Hayes
James A. Garfield	Ohio	1831–1881	1881	Republican	Lucretia Rudolph Garfield
Chester A. Arthur	Vermont	1829–1886	1881–1885	Republican	widower
Grover Cleveland	New Jersey	1837–1908	1885–1889	Democrat	Frances Folsom Cleveland

Our PRESIDENTS

President	Birthplace	Life Span	Presidency	Political Party	First Lady
Benjamin Harrison	Ohio	1833–1901	1889–1893	Republican	Caroline Scott Harrison
Grover Cleveland	New Jersey	1837–1908	1893–1897	Democrat	Frances Folsom Cleveland
William McKinley	Ohio	1843–1901	1897–1901	Republican	Ida Saxton McKinley
Theodore Roosevelt	New York	1858–1919	1901–1909	Republican	Edith Kermit Carow Roosevelt
William H. Taft	Ohio	1857–1930	1909–1913	Republican	Helen Herron Taft
Woodrow Wilson	Virginia	1856–1924	1913–1921	Democrat	Ellen L. Axson Wilson Edith Bolling Galt Wilson
Warren G. Harding	Ohio	1865–1923	1921–1923	Republican	Florence Kling De Wolfe Harding
Calvin Coolidge	Vermont	1872–1933	1923–1929	Republican	Grace Goodhue Coolidge
Herbert C. Hoover	Iowa	1874–1964	1929–1933	Republican	Lou Henry Hoover
Franklin D. Roosevelt	New York	1882–1945	1933–1945	Democrat	Anna Eleanor Roosevelt Roosevelt
Harry S. Truman	Missouri	1884–1972	1945–1953	Democrat	Elizabeth Wallace Truman

Our PRESIDENTS

President	Birthplace	Life Span	Presidency	Political Party	First Lady
Dwight D. Eisenhower	Texas	1890–1969	1953–1961	Republican	Mary "Mamie" Doud Eisenhower
John F. Kennedy	Massachusetts	1917–1963	1961–1963	Democrat	Jacqueline Bouvier Kennedy
Lyndon B. Johnson	Texas	1908–1973	1963–1969	Democrat	Claudia Alta Taylor Johnson
Richard M. Nixon	California	1913–1994	1969–1974	Republican	Thelma Catherine Ryan Nixon
Gerald Ford	Nebraska	1913–	1974–1977	Republican	Elizabeth "Betty" Bloomer Warren Ford
James Carter	Georgia	1924–	1977–1981	Democrat	Rosalynn Smith Carter
Ronald Reagan	Illinois	1911–	1981–1989	Republican	Nancy Davis Reagan
George Bush	Massachusetts	1924–	1989–1993	Republican	Barbara Pierce Bush
William Clinton	Arkansas	1946–	1993–2001	Democrat	Hillary Rodham Clinton
George W. Bush	Connecticut	1946–	2001–	Republican	Laura Welch Bush

Presidential FACTS

Qualifications
To run for president, a candidate must
- be at least 35 years old
- be a citizen who was born in the United States
- have lived in the United States for 14 years

Term of Office
A president's term of office is four years. No president can stay in office for more than two terms.

Election Date
The presidential election takes place every four years on the first Tuesday of November.

Inauguration Date
Presidents are inaugurated on January 20.

Oath of Office
I do solemnly swear I will faithfully execute the office of the President of the United States and will to the best of my ability preserve, protect, and defend the Constitution of the United States.

Write a Letter to the President
One of the best things about being a U.S. citizen is that Americans get to participate in their government. They can speak out if they feel government leaders aren't doing their jobs. They can also praise leaders who are going the extra mile. Do you have something you'd like the president to do? Should the president worry more about the environment and encourage people to recycle? Should the government spend more money on our schools? You can write a letter to the president to say how you feel!

1600 Pennsylvania Avenue
Washington, D.C. 20500

You can even send an e-mail to: president@whitehouse.gov

For Further INFORMATION

Internet Sites

Find links to James A. Garfield Web sites:
http://www.interlink-cafe.com/uspresidents/20th.htm

Find a children's listing of Civil War sites:
http://www.kidinfo.com/American_History/Civil_War.html

Read Garfield's inaugural speech:
http://www.bartleby.com/124/pres.36.html

Read more about Garfield's religious life and education:
http://www.mun.ca/rels/restmov/texts/jtbrown/coc/COC1306.HTM

See pictures and read about the James A. Garfield National Historic Site:
http://www.wrhs.org/sites/garfield.htm

Read more about Alexander Graham Bell and the Garfield assassination:
http://www.historybuff.com/library/refgarfield.html

Learn more about all the presidents and visit the White House:
http://www.whitehouse.gov/WH/glimpse/presidents/html/presidents.html
http://www.thepresidency.org/presinfo.htm
http://www.americanpresidents.org/

Books

Feinberg, Barbara Jane. *Electing the President.* New York: Twenty-First Century Books, 1995.

Graham, Martin F., Richard A. Sauers, and George Skoch. *The Blue and the Gray.* Lincolnwood, IL: Publications International, 1996.

Heinrichs, Ann. *Lucretia Rudolph Garfield: 1832–1918.* Chicago: Childrens Press, 1998.

Lester, Julius. *To Be a Slave.* New York: Scholastic, 1968.

Lillegard, Dee. *James A. Garfield: Twentieth President of the United States.* Chicago: Childrens Press, 1987.

Suid, Murray I. *How to Be President of the U.S.A.* Palo Alto, CA: Monday Morning Books, 1999.

Index